Welcome
to Confusion

A Surprising Doorway to God

Welcome
to Confusion

A Surprising Doorway to God

Barbara M. Russo

Adoration Publishing Company
Denver, Colorado USA

Adoration Pulishing Company
3767 South Jasmine Street
Denver CO 80237 USA
www.adorationpublishing.com

Welcome to Confusion: A Surprising Doorway to God
ISBN: 978-0-9822464-6-7 (print)
          978-0-9822464-7-4 (digital)

Suggested cataloging within the Library of Congress System

Russo, Barbara M.
Spiritual life—Christianity/Hidden God/Jesus Christ—Meditations
BV4501.3 .R87 2016
Library of Congress Control Number: 2016941994

Dewey Decimal Cataloging
Religion/Christian life and practice
248.4 R87 2016

For Blake Russo
1948–2013

Every question is a door-handle.

George MacDonald, *The Laird's Inheritance*

CONTENTS

ONE

The Gods Must Be Crazy

The Gods Must Be Crazy[1] is a cult film classic about a tiny band of !Kung Bushmen living in the Kalahari Desert. One day they see a glass coke bottle fall from the sky. Isolated from western ways, the Bushmen have no idea what this puzzling object could be, but it doesn't take them long to discover dozens of ingenious uses for it—none involving liquid refreshment. The new tool softens snakeskins and makes music. At first, everyone in the group wants personal time with the helpful gadget.

Yet, bit by bit the coke bottle changes the way the Bushmen feel about life. Arguments and bickering replace their old camaraderie, and the world becomes much more complicated. Before the coke bottle crashes into their lives, the Bushmen believe in gods who are good and kind. Afterwards, the Bushmen wonder if they've misjudged the gods. They decide that the gods must be crazy to have sent them such a disruptive and upsetting thing.

At heart, we are all Kalahari Bushmen. By early adulthood most of us feel that we have finally figured out life. We know that certain behaviors and beliefs are worthwhile and if we live by them, eventually the good things we deserve will happen. We are smart. The universe is predictable. The gods (whatever that may mean to us) are benign.

But sooner or later, bewildering coke bottles rain down on our heads. Our lives collapse in ways we couldn't have imagined. Perhaps we make choices we once thought were out of the question. We wake up one day sensing that the ground we've been standing on all these years is heaving.

I lowered myself into the pew after the church service ended and looked around. I saw friends chatting in small groups. I noticed the altar, arrayed in emerald green and gold fabrics. The altar was the center of our worship space, the place where my son's adoption had been blessed, where I had been confirmed, and where we celebrated weekly communion. But what captured my attention that morning was a plain wooden pillar between the window aisle and the pews. I stared vacantly at the post, not wanting to think or feel, when a picture came to my mind of my former self worshiping in the nearby seats.

I wearily told God, "I don't know why I keep coming. If a friend treated me this way I would be smart enough to let them go. But I'm still here, talking to you. I just don't know why anymore."

I was a church leader, a seminary student and a bible teacher. During my fifteen adult years of following Christ, I had encountered the presence of God in profound ways. But my experience of life no longer jibed with what I understood about God. I'd been through hard times before, but this was different.

I had reached the end of my rope and the future in front of me was dark. God had not answered my prayers. Trying to be responsive to his leading, I had used all my thinking and strategizing skills. I had done my best to stay flexible and make responsible choices. Now a new obstacle was beyond my control. I had lost my dream and the collateral damage was my sense of self. Logic told me the only explanation was that God did not want me anymore.

Talking to Christians made things worse. If I tried to express what I was going through, people either tried to talk me out of it, pray me out of it, or confess me out of it. Platitudes like "this must be God's will" and "whatever doesn't kill you makes you stronger" offered me no hope and sparked a resentment I did not want to feel. I felt shrugged off by people and tossed aside by God.

It was horrible to think I was wrong about myself, my place in the universe, and my ideas about life. Were the gods going crazy? And would I?

To ask oneself that question as a person of faith is deeply disturbing. If you are anything like me, you will probably feel like you are sliding toward unbelief and that there is something wrong with you. How to cope? What to do? At this point none of the possible choices will make life easy; many are even self-destructive. Will you retrench and become more rigid in your old ways of seeing? Will you lash out in rage? Will you numb out on an addiction of choice? Will you throw up your hands and walk away? Or will you find a bigger way of seeing reality, of understanding the God Who Is? This last choice is the most life-giving, but is also the most terrifying. In this direction there is no clear path, and everyone has to find a way through their own confusing labyrinth of questions and dead-ends.

Through the centuries, faithful people have continued to experience perplexing coke bottle moments with God. After one particularly trying day, St. Teresa of Avila, the sixteenth century mystic, is reputed to have said to God, "Well if this is how you treat your friends, no wonder you have so few of them!" Everyone would prefer to understand how God works and to feel that they are on solid ground. We all want life to make sense. Certainly there are seasons and times for that. But other seasons, less desired, may be even more important.

Only those who submit to seasons of unknowing, like St. Teresa, will be open enough to receive visions of God as he really is. Only people who know they need healing can be healed. That is why bewilderment about God does not have to be regarded as a defect to be suppressed. It can be received as a doorway.

Yet however pious that sounds, the fact is we all have to be dragged or pushed up to that doorway. We may long for transformation, but no one (certainly not me) eagerly embraces the arduous path that leads there. Consequently, when we see Jesus pushing and prodding earnest spiritual people into uncertainty and confusion, perhaps we should not be surprised. Apparently Jesus went about the country dropping coke bottles onto people's heads!

The events narrated here are grounded in Scripture and history. The thoughts and feelings of those who encountered Jesus belong to us all.

Journaling Starter

Have you ever felt that your "gods" were going crazy? What was that like for you?

Jesus said,
"As for these things that you see,
the days will come when not one stone
will be left upon another;
all will be thrown down."

Luke 21:6

TWO

Unimaginable Tomorrows

I've visited Washington D.C. three times in my life. I am a history junkie and Washington is to me like a steak dinner to a hungry man. I long to devour everything. Though my trips have never been extensive enough to allow me to see all I want, each time I find myself spending precious hours returning to four compelling monuments. I was born a cynic, but I don't feel cynical when I stand in the shadow of the Lincoln Memorial, the Jefferson Memorial, the White House, or Arlington National Cemetery. Experiencing these four places is like listening to our country's heartbeat. For the moments I am there it seems as if all our national dysfunction has been transcended and that I have come into the presence of the very best of us.

Most Americans have a visceral attachment to the National Mall, particularly the White House. The White House is Us. It is our heritage, our identity, our past and our future. For the Jews of Jesus' time, their temple meant all of that and, even more, it meant the awe-inspiring presence of God.

Jesus' disciples, like all the people of first century Palestine, were living in their own kind of post 9/11, dog-eat-dog world, trying to stay out of the way of some brutal Roman soldier, and struggling to keep their families fed. One day the disciples go for a walk with Jesus through the temple grounds. Like the Galilean tourists they are, they chatter to Jesus, "Look at this beautiful building. Isn't this fantastic? Haven't they done a nice job of decorating now that it's finally finished after all these decades? Did you know that just one of these building stones weighs fifteen tons? How do you suppose they moved them into place?"

The temple dominates the city skyline, fifteen stories tall, plated with gold. Its construction is an incredible accomplishment for a poor little country in the backwash of the Roman Empire. This gorgeous achievement stands for God's blessing and ultimate victory. The temple is their sense of security and national identity while living under Roman occupation. It means that despite their troubles, God is still with them.

Life is hard, so for just a few minutes the disciples want to feel that the world has stability and order and predictability. A world where beautiful things get built, and stay built, and you can count on tomorrow. They want to look at this temple glinting in the sunshine and feel that God's in his heaven and all's right with the world.

Knowing that Jesus is into God and stuff, they expect him to be excited too. After all, this is the temple; this is the place where God is. This is where you go if you really want to experience God. And what does Jesus do? He bursts their bubble. He spoils their fun. He says, "Someday not even one stone of this building will be left standing."

This is practically treason and nearly blasphemy. If the temple were to be destroyed, God's honor would go with it. It is unthinkable. God just wouldn't—couldn't—allow that to happen.

Despite their innocent intentions, Jesus won't let the disciples pretend that everything is nice and sweet when it isn't. He reminds them that you can't count on tomorrow, at least not the tomorrow that depends on buildings, and governments, and good salaries, and plenty of everything. You can't even count on your way of life or your religious habits or philosophical systems. Not in his age, not in our age, not in any age.

Jesus interrupted the world of the disciples the way life sometimes interrupts us. Life interrupts with lost jobs, bad health, spoiled dreams, and sometimes even disaster. Life teaches us that we live in a world where anything can happen. All the things we think could never be, might be. We have visceral attachments to our ideas about the way life works, and who God is. We stand on visions of reality that may be as beautiful, and as temporary, as the temple in Jerusalem.

When I left my home in Colorado to get my Masters of Divinity degree in Pittsburgh, I was absolutely certain that since I was saying yes to what God had given me to do, I would be able to flourish in the doing of it. When someone expressed concern that as a woman I might have a hard time getting a pastoral job, I remember thinking, "God won't let that happen to me." But it turned out that I was wrong about my life and wrong about God.

Standing in the temple with his disciples, Jesus knows they haven't got a clue about reality. He's certain that Rome will inevitably plunder and destroy Jerusalem's temple, and he senses that his own arrest and crucifixion are imminent. He knows that doubts, despair, persecutions and heart wrenching times lie ahead for the disciples. He wants them to wake up to reality, and he knows they need to wake up fast. He wants them to see the truth the way God sees it. He wants them to grow the inner spiritual resources they will need for what life will demand of them.

Waking up to reality doesn't just mean realizing that misfortune and heartbreak might happen. Waking up to reality also means realizing that our explanations and impressions about life and about God are constructs, every bit as much as the temple. When it was built, the temple was the most authentic demonstration of God's nature yet possible, the most perfect place to worship him, but even so it was not the same as God himself.

Human beings love beauty and symmetry. With our hands we construct beautiful and symmetrical monuments. With our heads we construct beautiful and symmetrical philosophies and doctrines. There is nothing inappropriate about this, for our constructs help us express our yearnings and comfort our hearts with the beauty and symmetry of God. But Jesus' warning to the disciples also stands as a warning to us, for "one day there will not be a stone left of all this."

When our philosophies about God come to mean more to us than God himself, then we are headed inexorably for doubt and disillusionment. No system of thought or logic, not even any depth of feeling, can perfectly contain the beauty and symmetry of God. Even so, there will be times in life when God seems neither beautiful nor symmetrical, when the disconnect between our suppositions about God and our experience of God is so vast that we are tempted to say there is no reality or beauty to God at all.

Even the wisest and most careful among us will have added embellishments, or even whole cross-beams and joists to our understanding of God that cannot bear weight. And when the rafters begin to fall in on us through the burdens of life, or the weakness of our own inflexible reasoning, then we may despair that God himself has only been a house of cards.

Waking up to reality means putting our hope not in a construct, but in the invisible Beauty who remains, even when everything we are standing on gets ripped away. Within a generation of Jesus' prediction, when all that survived of the temple was the Wailing Wall, God's beauty did not vanish from the world. It remains to this day, hovering over us. It remains tangible in the person of the crucified and resurrected Jesus, even if—or when—the unimaginable happens.

Journaling Starter

Have any of your earlier assumptions about life disappointed you? In what ways have your views of God changed as a result?

Now there was a Pharisee named Nicodemus,

a leader of the Jews.

He came to Jesus by night.

John 3:1–2

THREE

Running on Empty

I have no memory of the first time I heard the phrase "born again." The words were not common fare in my household. We did not watch Billy Graham Crusades on TV or go to revivals on Saturday nights. Nevertheless, "born again" was in the air.

My first exposure to the words "born again" probably happened while I stared out the rear window of our family Ford. Every county road displayed at least one billboard proclaiming that I *must* be born again. I had no idea what the billboards wanted me to do, but whatever it was, it made me mad.

I didn't like anyone telling me I had to do anything.

When the internet came along I discovered that I could buy born-again vitamins and surfboards, study born-again planets and join bornagainrebels.com. Born again continues to be part of the American cultural landscape. Often a laughable part.

But the night Nicodemus encountered Jesus it was the first time anyone, anywhere had heard of "born again."

It wasn't laughable at all.

It was shocking.

Nicodemus was the best of the best of the spiritual best. He was on the board of directors of Pharisees United and had a bundle of influence and cash at his disposal. He was paying Jesus a big compliment by coming to see him at all, even if it was in the middle of the night (so the other board members wouldn't find out). He was sure Jesus would be grateful—probably ask him for some pointers about getting back on the good side of the central power brokers. But Jesus didn't even say thanks for coming. He didn't ask for advice. He just dropped the coke bottle: "So you want to see the kingdom of God. You need to be conceived by

God's spirit, born-again." (If Nicodemus had been in the zone, he would have heard Jesus saying "You think you have the inside track to God. You don't." Maybe he did hear it and couldn't believe Jesus would say that, not to *him*.)

Sensing he was losing control of the conversation, Nicodemus tried to spin things back his way, take Jesus down a peg. "What in the world are you talking about? Nobody can be conceived after they're already born and old." Jesus cut to the chase. "All you get from being descended from Abraham is more Abraham-stuff. He was flesh and blood, and flesh can only produce more flesh, nothing new. Being of God's spirit is something different than all your pedigreed insider garbage. You don't understand the wind either, do you? But it blows just the same." Nicodemus was feeling pretty disoriented by then. "What *are* you talking about?"

When I was young the idea that God existed did not impress me. If God was doing anything for the world, you could have fooled me. It was clear to me that ancient people had invented the idea of gods to meet their own needs. I didn't mind if modern people wanted to buy into that, just so long as none of them expected me to do the same.

Yet much to my surprise, a few years down the road I had an experience of Jesus that convinced me a loving God was real. I was grateful to have been found by God and his grace. I wanted to hear more about him, so church seemed like the logical place to go.

At church I learned to work hard at being spiritual. It was fun and interesting. I did good things for God; he did good things for me. It seemed like a fine arrangement that made a lot of sense. Without recanting any of my convictions about God's love and grace, I started believing that I had the correct spiritual answers; the right spiritual practices and belonged to the best spiritual community. I started believing God got a pretty sweet deal when I signed up. Without even noticing it was happening, the big religious outsider (me) morphed into a religious insider.

Once you are a religious insider it is all too easy to suppose that your knowledge, your status and your many sacrifices are the reason God showers you with blessings, answers your prayers, and seats you near his right hand. But being a spiritual person is not at its core about knowing the right answers, coming from the right family, having the right practices, or joining the right community. Being of God's spirit, conceived from God, isn't a spiritual *accomplishment* at all.

This is the coke bottle Jesus dropped on Nicodemus. If you know as much as Nicodemus and you've been as good as he is, as devoted as he is, as important as he is, then you're pretty sure that God needs you, not the other way around. When you've been as religious as Nicodemus, it's your list of virtues, not your shortcomings that mess up your connection with God.

Contrary to what so many of us were taught, the opposite of faith is not doubt, but self-sufficiency. The only deliverance from self-sufficiency is through disorientation. That's what Jesus is trying to do for Nicodemus—so he spins Nicodemus around and makes him wonder which direction is up. Pushes him to realize that even though he knows a lot about God, his heart is empty. Maybe if Nick gets disoriented enough, he will start struggling to be born into a new way of seeing and a new way of being. A way of being empty that is full of God's life instead of a way of being full that is completely empty.

Journaling Starter

Have your spiritual accomplishments ever interfered with your connection to God? Have you ever been too self-sufficient for your own good?

A leper came to him begging him,
and kneeling he said to him,
"If you choose, you can make me clean."

Mark 1:40

FOUR

Risking Wholeness

Is everyone today obsessed with germs? I am old enough to remember a time before soap promised to kill bacteria on my hands, before spray cleaners vowed to kill viruses on my kitchen counters. I can even remember plain water, before it was purified and put into bottles to get me to drink it. Nevertheless, I have so totally bought into this thing about germs, that now I wash my hands while singing my ABCs, to ensure that the microorganisms float down the sink to germ nirvana.

We Americans are probably more preoccupied with avoiding contamination than any people since the ancient Hebrews.

The Hebrew people didn't worry about contagious bugs that might lead to a few days in bed or even a visit to the emergency room. Instead, they worried about soul contamination, about infections of the spirit. So they avoided places and people that carried contagious soul diseases. To them, one of the worst of these soul toxins was leprosy.

Untreated leprosy is still a terrifying disease. It damages nerve endings and deadens physical pain. People with leprosy can't tell when they hurt themselves because they feel no pain. They can't tell when vermin gnaw at their fingers because they have no sensations in their extremities. One wound on top of another, and soon lepers begin to lose parts of themselves to infections. First the fingers and toes go, then the earlobes and noses, and then more and more parts.

In ancient Israel, leprosy was dreaded. Fear meant that, to be on the safe side, anyone with a skin disease or a rash was considered a leper. Only a priest could certify that the problem had cleared up. If you noticed a sore spot, your physical problems would be the least of your worries. You'd become an outcast required to yell out "unclean, unclean" as a warning to passersby. You would have to keep fifty steps away from everyone, even from the few friends and family who might want to risk visiting you.

Everyone knew that anyone with leprosy was spiritually contaminated and cut off from God. Fifty steps made good plain sense. Because if a leper touched you, you would become spiritually cut off too, dismembered from the source of goodness.

The leper sitting by the side of the road stares blankly toward Capernaum. This leper once had a name, but now is just called *the leper who sits on the road to Capernaum.* He remembers his name, his wife, his baby son, his work—all of his earlier life, now dismembered. But these thoughts are painful, too painful.

Clamp down on those memories fast, he orders himself. *That* life vanished overnight. You can still walk, but that will go too. And maybe sooner would be better than later. Just get it over with and die. No, think of something else. Remember yesterday, someone

hollering about a man, a prophet maybe, who was healing people. But so what? What good would it do, even
if a prophet really had cured some sick people? Lepers
have been abandoned by God—everybody knows that.
If this prophet truly is from God, then he has to stay
away from lepers. No point in dreaming about healing.
Besides, too much hope is dangerous. If the prophet
turned his back, that would be total blackness, worse
than no hope. So it's better just to rot on the road to
Capernaum.

Oh? Better for who? Better for the baby, for her?
What will happen to them? Begging, that's what. Oh,
God!

God, please, no!

What if you could see her and the baby again,
not from far away, like a walking ghost, but like a man,
look after them? Maybe the prophet would help, after
all? What if you could find this prophet somehow? Not
for you, but for them.

For the baby. For *her*.

One day a ragged leper hobbles through a crowd, heading toward Jesus. People standing nearby gasp, back away, mutter angrily. *What a dirt bag—he knows the rules—doesn't he care about infecting people—or about infecting Jesus!* The leper keeps coming, eyes straight ahead. Then his eyes lock on the eyes of Jesus. Fifty steps away…keep going. Then forty. Step again.

Jesus doesn't move, barely breathes. His eyes never leave the eyes of the quarantined outcast limping toward him.

Abruptly staggered by what he is risking, the leper throws himself to the ground. Head in the dust, he chokes out, "Oh, Lord if you are willing, you can make me clean." His sense of nothingness presses him down, keeps him there.

Jesus' lips tighten with anger. *Serves that leper right,* the crowd thinks. They lean forward to hear the harsh reprimand Jesus will impose. But Jesus, the prophet from God, squats down in the dust and lays a determined hand on the man's shoulder.

Despising suffering, hating nature's indifference, devoted to giving wholeness, Jesus roars, "I am willing. Be clean!"

If, like the leper on the road to Capernaum, we can bear to be honest with our souls, most of us will sense a yearning for something more than life has handed us.

Your yearning might be a longing for connection, intimacy. It might be a hunger for becoming who you are meant to be. Other times it might be a nagging feeling that there is a missing piece you can't find words for. You might ache for beauty, for something wonderful that is just out of reach. Or, you may not be able to feel anything at all, as if your soul has gone away and won't come home. Emptiness is its own terrible kind of yearning.

Being honest with ourselves can take us into awareness of our pain, our incompleteness and our vulnerability. We are not whole, and we feel it.

We are all lepers in our souls.

As dreadful as that sounds, and as true as it is, we are not ruined. Like the Capernaum leper, we can discover the Absolute Wholeness which fills the unseen dimension beyond this one and refuses to abandon us. Small foretastes of wholeness reach our side of reality and feed our souls. These glimpses of wholeness, along with our aching incompleteness, are powerful reminders that we are designed for union, for wholeness, and for fullness.

Ironically, our very sensitivity to our incomplete condition is a reason for hope. In my experience, poignant desires for wholeness mean I am drawing closer to its source, not moving further away. The closer I am to my husband, the more I want to be closer still; the closer I am to God, the deeper my longing for him becomes; and the more fully I am in touch with my soul, the more I want to become all I am meant to be. In fact, one of the first signs that a person is on a new path toward wholeness will be a capacity to experience pain again. We need to reflect that after Jesus healed a leper, the pain came back.

Many people expect that their faith or emotional maturity should be great enough to prevent any sense of incompleteness and emptiness, but this is unrealistic and can lead to crippling shame. It is all too easy to assume that everyone else is perfectly fine, but something disgraceful is wrong with me. To escape a gnawing sense of deformity, some of us numb our souls with addictive obsessions and distractions. And although we are not forced to keep fifty paces away from everyone, we still find ways to keep others at a distance—so no one can guess how empty and weak we really are. Before long, our numbing and hiding behavior pushes us even further away from the source of wholeness.

Even so, we lepers have hope. There is a way toward wholeness, but it requires the courage of the leper who sought out Jesus. It will ask us to value, not reject, our aching longing for wholeness. We will be called on to see our incomplete soul as it really is. We will be challenged to reveal our most authentic, innermost parts to God, and to let him touch our souls.

Curiously, the soul is somewhat like a lobster. Though lobsters are protected by their shells, their shells cannot get any bigger. Each time a lobster grows, it must crawl out of its old, safe shell and wait defenseless on the ocean floor. This happens many times during a lobster's long life. Likewise, for us, soul-wholeness is a life-long journey. Constricting shells (such as pretension, needing to be needed, or power-hunger) will have to be discarded along the way. On this soulful journey, we can expect to grow out of our shells and be made vulnerable to God's touch, not just one time, but again and again.

Like the leper, if we courageously accept the challenges of a journey toward wholeness, the way itself will begin to transform us. Our hesitating steps will take us in the direction of Jesus. We will grow toward God and toward others. We will develop a greater capacity to seek and receive spiritual beauty. We will become people who experience life with all its joy and pain. We will live into our destiny.

Journaling Starter

What does wholeness mean to you? What shells have trapped your soul and kept you from growing? What frightens you the most about the journey toward wholeness?

.

"Unless I see the mark of the nails in his hands,
and put my finger in the mark of the nails
and my hand in his side,
I will not believe."

John 20:25

FIVE

Doubting to Believe

The summer I turned twelve, my parents sent me to confirmation class. I was no believer, but I went willingly enough, saying to myself, "Finally, a chance to ask my questions and get some straight answers. Or at least some useful give-and-take." That's not quite how it turned out. Decades later my father revealed to me that one of the class directors had called him and demanded that my dad make me stop asking questions. (I must get some of my stubbornness from him, because he never bowed to the pressure to hush me up.) By the end of the week, all I remember thinking is that these church people seemed awfully defensive, so they must not be very secure about their ideas. I concluded that if they didn't have any confidence in this nonsense, there was no reason for me to buy into it. I announced to my parents that I didn't believe in religion, wasn't getting confirmed and was <u>never</u> going back to church.

My parents were speechless.

God laughed up his sleeve.

Personally, I don't think God minds questions. I think he likes them. And I think he has a soft spot for skeptics who actually want to know what's going on. That's the kind of skeptic I was when I was twelve—I only wanted to know what was real.

Afterwards, and for several years, I became a member of the guild of perpetual skepticism. I disbelieved everything, all the time, just on principle. During this stage, I wasn't sure it was even *possible* to know anything. I might not even have believed the world was round, except that I had seen the pictures taken from space. Though I had no assertions of my own to defend, I had no trouble poking holes in everyone else's suppositions and speculations. Poking holes helped me keep potential disillusionment at arm's length. Disbelief became a safe and emotionally detached refuge from a complex world. It was less risky to park myself permanently on doubt than to chance the ups and downs of an earnest quest.

After years of disdain, when I started honestly searching for spiritual reality, life got much scarier. Reconsidering what you know about life will make you feel as if the ground is shaking under your feet. During an earthquake there's no place to stand, nothing to hide under, and a lot of mess to clean up when it's over. To come through a spiritual earthquake, you have to live with a lot of anxiety and disarray for a while.

Take Thomas, one of the first followers of Jesus. Thomas was never going to be bait for some scammer selling farmland on the shores of the Dead Sea, or some anonymous Greek widow giving away ten million drachmas through an email address. People call him "Doubting Thomas" because he wanted evidence before he changed his whole way of seeing things. But there was more going on inside Thomas than just obstinate disbelief.

Thomas was committed to the God of Israel. That's why he became a disciple. More than a follower of Jesus, he was a staunch friend, the soul of devotion.

Shortly before Jesus' death, when Jesus insisted on going to Jerusalem, and everyone else was trying to talk Jesus out of it, Thomas said OK, since he's so set on going, let's go and die with him. Yet, when the terrible moment arrived, Thomas was missing in action, just like the rest of them. Along with the others, the crucifixion threw him into a tailspin. What he thought he knew about himself, he didn't. What he thought he would do, he couldn't. What he thought he understood about God, he hadn't. Wracked with terror, grief, guilt and despair, he had to start from scratch, not sure about anyone or anything, not sure about himself, not sure about God.

Yet, after Jesus' execution, Thomas tries to pick up the pieces of his life and go on. Maybe that's why he wasn't there when the other disciples encountered the resurrected Jesus. Whatever the reason, when the disciples tell Thomas their outrageous story about Jesus being alive, even though everyone in Jerusalem knows the Master is dead and buried, it is clear to Thomas that they have all cracked under the pressure or they are playing a tasteless joke on him. If I had been Thomas,

I might have stormed out in anger at that point, pretty near the edge of what I could bear. Thomas doesn't storm out.

Maybe hearing this far-fetched story from his closest friends, knowing they've been through a lot lately, makes him bite his tongue and listen to what they have to say. Yet, after a few hours, they still aren't making any sense to him. His friends don't appear to be crazy (well, any crazier than they've ever been), but for some baffling reason they seem to honestly believe Jesus is alive. Not like a wraith or a zombie, not like a mirage or a memory, not even like a hologram, but alive in the flesh. Not dead anymore, but different, changed, enhanced somehow.

Thomas knows that it ought to go without saying that if someone is literally, truly dead on Friday, they stay literally, truly dead on Sunday. This is not brain surgery. Even so, he can't convince everyone that they've fallen for some horrible scam that will scandalize them when they come to their senses. Thomas doesn't take the nice way out and tell them he's sure the resurrection is true for *them,* just not true for *him.* He is adamant that he won't toss his common sense into the river the way the rest of Jesus' disciples apparently have. He insists, "Unless I see the mark of the nails in his hands, and put my finger in the mark of the nails and my hand in his side, I will not believe." Thomas gets in touch with his reservations, owns them, and doesn't let anybody convince him to shrug them off.

He could keep quiet about his doubts and maintain the peace. He could make light of his issues, but instead he hangs on to them. Thomas could go looking for a new group of friends who will tell him he is right and the disciples are the loony ones. He doesn't do that either.

As the poet Rainer Maria Rilke once urged, Thomas lived the questions. He made the challenging choice to live his questions with people who didn't believe the way he did, but who supported his journey, who weren't threatened by his questions and who let him wonder and wait.

After about a week of this stalemate, when they are all together again, Jesus shows up. He shows up in spite of solid walls, nervous energy, and locked doors.

Jesus doesn't need anyone to tell him what Thomas has been thinking. Jesus gently says, "Put your finger here and consider my hands. Put your hand to my side. Do not go on without faith, but believe."

Thomas never gets an explanation from Jesus about how the resurrection works. Instead of answers, Jesus gives Thomas *himself*—flesh and blood and wounds to touch. Thomas' doubts aren't overcome by philosophy or common sense, but by an encounter with Something beyond rational explanation.

In my own life, for over a year and a half, I looked for explanations, trying to decide if Christianity held together logically, if there could possibly be good reasons to believe. Eventually I concluded that the Christian religion was philosophically consistent, that it made sense. At the time, Christian philosophy was enough for me—but God knew I needed more. I needed to know in my gut that God is more than a nice idea, but a real Someone who is present, who labors, who hurts. I needed to encounter his reality for myself.

That's what Thomas needed. I like to think that because Thomas was on an earnest quest, not just poking holes in other people's ideas, God showed up.

Thomas doubted hard, he believed hard, he loved hard. Tradition tells us that Thomas made his way to India and founded the church there, telling the Christian story, dying a martyr's death. People like Thomas don't have easy lives. But they have lives crammed full of being alive. Passionate Thomas, always thinking for himself, was the first one in history to say to Jesus, "My Lord, and my God!" Despite the fact that the Jews had, and still have, a fierce aversion to idol worship, Jesus, the consummate Jew, accepted Thomas' insight that Jesus is somehow or other the very essence of God. Even though that epiphany contradicted everything Thomas had been taught and had believed for years, he gave up his death grip on the old perspective—and embraced a God who turned out to be even bigger than he imagined God could possibly be.

Journaling Starter

Are you naturally more skeptical or more trusting? How has that served you? Created difficulties?

What is your reaction to the phrase "live the questions"? Have you always felt that way?

As Jesus walked along,
he saw a man blind from birth.
His disciples asked him,
"Rabbi, who sinned, this man or his parents,
that he was born blind?"

John 9:1–2

SIX

In the Dark

Late one afternoon when my younger son Mark was about three years old we were curled up on the couch watching television with his older brother. Suddenly the TV screen popped, the lamps went out and we were plunged into total darkness. Mark shrieked with the terror of early humankind experiencing its first solar eclipse. His brother and I tried to reassure him that the lights would come back on and that he was OK. He couldn't hear us. With his reptilian brain in full swing, the screaming continued.

In the darkness, I felt my way around the coffee table, past the breakfast bar and into the kitchen. By the remains of the sunset trickling through the kitchen window, I located the flashlight and switched on its small circle of light. Only after Mark was able to discern familiar shapes and faces was he able to hear our words of reassurance and come back to his right mind.

When the lights went out, Mark's solid and predictable world collapsed. He was powerless to feel safe or whole until the catastrophe was put right. He didn't need to be ridiculed or rejected. He didn't need a lecture on electricity. He needed to see.

It was the Sabbath. I was sitting by the side of the temple road, like I always do, with my coat spread out under me to catch any coins travelers might throw to me. There hadn't been much traffic, so it was easy to sense a group of footsteps coming down the road from the temple. Minutes later came the matching voices, asking whether my parents broke God's rules and made me blind, or whether it was my fault. Most everyone swears somebody must have done something really bad for God to punish me like this, so I've heard that question more times than I care to remember. Once people figure out you're blind, they think you can't hear anything either. You get used to it.

But what I heard after that, I wasn't used to at all. Another voice answered that being blind wasn't my fault or anyone's fault. I admit I always thought God was pretty mean to punish me for something that happened before I was born, so I hoped the voice would say more. I stretched my ears toward the voices, but all I could make out were strange swishy sounds. Before long someone was plastering something soft and tingly on my eyes. I'm pretty sure that the swishy noise I heard was spitting, and the goo on my eyes was mud. It must have taken an impressive amount of spit! But before I could decide how I felt about that, the voice sent me to wash off my eyes in the big pool nearby.

I was wondering how I could get there when hands grabbed me and half-ran, half-lifted me along to the pool. On the way I asked the name of the mud-man and they said Jesus, but I didn't have time to find out more. The next thing I knew my face was in the water. By the time we got back to my spot by the road,

I didn't hear the mud-man's voice anymore. I guess he left, but I could <u>see</u>.

I didn't know what to do. My heart was pounding and everything felt strange and uncomfortable. Even so, I couldn't stop grinning. I started walking in circles, touching it all. The world is so pretty! I kneeled down to finger the dusty road and it was beautiful. I couldn't help crying. How did he do this? *Why* did he do this?

The best part was the colors, but it was hard to get used to all the shapes moving around. I had to close my eyes pretty often so I could understand what was happening. Another crazy thing, as soon as I could see <u>them</u>, my neighbors couldn't recognize <u>me</u>. It was as if my seeing made them go blind. I had to keep telling them it was really me.

Even so, everybody in the neighborhood wanted me to tell the story over and over. After a while they took me to some Pharisees who wanted to hear the whole report again, top to bottom. I told them the very same thing I told my neighbors, only I didn't exactly mention about the man making the mud on the Sabbath. I don't know much about the rules, but I think you aren't supposed to do things like that. I decided not to say anything about the spit either. I'm not sure where they stand on that part.

After I told my story, the Pharisees got in a big argument. Half of them said the mud-man must be from God, and the other half said he couldn't be from God or he would have waited until the next day to help me. Everybody was awfully upset, so I decided I would just go home. I've never been able to do that before.

Day after day, different Pharisees came to pester me with questions. The last time they came, they took me back to the synagogue and asked me what I thought about the mud-man. I liked what some of those Pharisees in that earlier group said, that only a prophet from God could heal someone born blind like me. So that's what I said too. But it didn't go over so well. Everyone in the place started yelling and arguing with me. Finally, they pushed me out of the synagogue onto the road and told me to never come back (like they ever wanted me coming in the first place). Some of those guys are nuts, really scary. I hope the mud-man watches out.

After a week or so, the mud-man came by to see me. I recognized his voice right away. I didn't expect him to visit; he didn't need to do that. But I am glad he came. Friendly visitors have pretty much dried up since the synagogue incident. People used to avoid me when I was blind, now they avoid me because I can see. Overall, life was a lot simpler before. I'm not complaining. It's just that I didn't know seeing would be so controversial and so much work.

Can you believe it, the mud-man is the first person since I've been able to see who wanted to have a conversation with me about something besides mud! While he was here he said he wasn't the mud-man but the Son of Man and that he came to help the blind see and show the seeing how blind they are. That sounds mixed up, but maybe it's not.

I've met a lot of people lately who can't seem to imagine God is anywhere but in their own opinions. And I've met a lot of people who are only willing to see who and what they've made up their mind to see.

Maybe if they were sure of less, they could see more. Maybe if Jesus plastered over their souls so they didn't know so much, he'd be doing them as big a favor as he did for me.

Don't get me wrong. Being able to see hasn't fixed all my problems. In fact, it's added some new ones. But I've discovered that there's a beautiful world inside me that I never knew existed. Jesus didn't only light up my eyes, he lit up my soul. I wouldn't trade that away, even if I had to go blind again to keep it.

Journaling Starter

What parts of the blind man's experiences do you identify with the most?

Has being sure of less ever helped you see more?

The young man said to Jesus,
"I have kept all these; what do I still lack?"

Matthew 19:20

SEVEN

Dancing on Air

Cirque Du Soleil, acrobatic theater, was made for people like me. When I was a little girl, I loved to go to the circus. Though I hated seeing animals locked in tiny cages, and cotton candy was a big disappointment, all the noise and dirt and smell was worth it, if I could see the trapeze artists. In their glitzy costumes, they would climb a rope ladder to a tiny platform way up near the top of the circus tent. Then they would raise one arm to salute the crowd and swing out on a bar, until halfway through the air they would let go. Let go, and fall toward an empty bar swinging at them from the opposite platform. But rather than drop, they danced in the air.

The young CEO in the crowd that winter day in Judea was handsome, he was bright, he was rich. He'd been to the right schools and he always knew just what to do and say. (Nowadays he'd be running for Congress.) He certainly knew how to approach the rich and famous, having done it so many times.

———

Deftly making his way toward the center of the crowd, the young man lingers in the crush of people gathered around Jesus, waiting for his chance. As soon as Jesus finishes talking and turns to walk away, the twenty-something executive seizes the moment. Darting in front of Jesus, he falls to his knees and speaks his carefully composed question, "Good teacher, what should I do if I want eternal life?"

Jesus looks at this Prince Charming and sizes him up. Sometimes these sorts of people get on Jesus' nerves. Young, privileged, used to getting what he wants from people but…something else.

Jesus snaps out, "Why do you call me good? No one is good but God alone." Surprised and confused, the executive, whose name happens to be Ari, is momentarily at a loss for words. This isn't how the game is played. You always start with flattery to make them appreciate you.

Jesus allows Ari only a beat of silence to respond. Then he tersely recites for Ari the answer every Jew in Israel already accepts. "You know the commandments. Let me give you the Cliff Notes version. No killing, adultery, stealing, lying about people or defrauding them; honor your parents, treat people right."

Ari senses familiar ground at last. This is his chance to regain control of the conversation. He says, "Well teacher, I've done all that since I was small."

At this point Ari's mentors normally gush, "Ah Ari, God is with you. So young, and already so impressive. Maybe we can get you a scholarship to study in Jerusalem." Ari imagines how pleased Jesus will be with his answer. "Really? *All* the commandments? Since you were a child? That's amazing! You are way ahead of these country bumpkins I've got hanging about." Then, sensing Ari's worth, Jesus will look at the crowd and say, "Everyone, listen! This is the most righteous son of Israel I have ever met." *That* would feel good. Yes, hearing from Jesus could be just the thing to shore him up, remind him he's on track for Eternity, if anyone is. Then maybe that niggling uneasiness in his gut that something is still missing might finally go away.

For most of us, the phrase "eternal life" implies immortality in some extremely pleasant place. (The Romans called it the Elysian Fields, and the Norse called it Valhalla.) Perhaps this is how the rich young man thought about it too. The assumption was (and is) that the good-life-ever-after is the same as the good-life-in-the-here-and-now, only more so. But eternal life is not primarily about ongoing enjoyable experiences after you die. It's not really about immortality at all. At least, that's not the way Jesus and the first Christians talked and wrote about it. Eternal life is a different sort of life altogether, a life of deep connectedness with God and, accordingly, with one's most real and spiritual self. That sort of connectedness can never die. That sort of life will never end.

Spiritual connectedness is not a prize, an accessory, to carry around in our arms. In fact, the fuller our arms are with the regalia of life, the harder it will be to grab hold of the actual source of life. Success, wealth and prestige can so fill our arms and hearts that our capacity to connect to the biggest and most important things withers away. Even something as wonderful as family can leave too little room for kinship with God and with yourself. The chance to deeply connect to God and to our most authentic self begins, not with adding on, but with letting go.

Jesus gives Ari one long piercing look. He sees past all the arrogance and insecurity, past the self-absorption, and puts his finger on something in Ari that flickers on and off. How to give Ari a chance? A chance to get out of the sticky web of spiritualized status, prosperity, and self-indulgence he's wrapped himself in, a chance to come alive to the person God created him to be. "You are only missing one thing. Go sell everything you have, give it to the poor and you will have treasures in heaven. Then come and follow me."

Tossing the trapeze bar toward Ari, Jesus yells, "Swing it back!" Stunned, Ari pushes the bar toward Jesus and Jesus catches it, rolls up and over the bar, swings and lands back on the little platform high above the ground. "Want to try?" And he pushes the bar back toward Ari.

Jesus waits in the silence, hoping.

Standing on a tiny platform high in the air, Ari stares down at the plummet.

Let go? If I sell everything, no one will be able to tell how good I am or how important I've become. People won't have any way to see how much God approves of me. Plus, it will be next to impossible to keep up God's standards, if I'm wandering around the country, eating God knows what, running into God knows who. That can't be good. And if I go away to follow Jesus, I'll just be a nobody in a group of nobody's. Worst of all, once I give everything away, I can't change my mind if it doesn't work out. I could never go back.

The bar swings slower in the air.
Jesus gives it another push.
A chance to break through the sticky web to freedom,
dance in the air.
The bar stops swinging and Jesus sighs.
Not today. Not for Ari.

No one comes to God hoping for a chance to let go. Most of us come for practical help or for reassurance or to sense that we are loved. We do not come looking for an opportunity to live without safe, secure answers about life and God. We don't come intending to learn that what we think we know, we don't; and that who we think we are we aren't. Receiving a chance to let go, instead of what we came looking for, is at the very least unappealing, and frequently terrifying.

Like Ari, most of us prefer to back away slowly.

But if we back away, we won't discover the bigger life, the bigger God and the spiritual wholeness we have been longing for. If we dare to loosen our grip we may discover that letting go isn't falling, but dancing on air.

Journaling Starter

Have you ever had a life-giving experience with letting go? What scares you the most about letting go?

The apostles said to the Lord,
"Increase our faith!"

Luke 17:5

EIGHT

Small Is the New Big

America has gone mad for superheroes and superpowers. In case you haven't been counting, more than sixty superhero movies have been released in the past decade, and thirty more are scheduled for production. The mania isn't limited to the movies. If you are a gamer, part of the draw is choosing the special powers your avatar will command.

There's no doubt that the fantasy worlds of superheroes are full of adventure and action. But fun escapism isn't their only appeal. Like us, superheroes confront intractable problems and injustice. Unlike us, they aren't overwhelmed and helpless in the face of such things. Instead, superheroes confront annihilating forces and come out on top. Superheroes *do* something when no one else can. While the real world all too often makes us feel small, superpower fantasies make us feel big. It's make-believe as old as humankind.

———

Three men wander and stoop, gathering kindling for the fire. Trails of pink meander across the twilight sky.

One of the men sighs. "Remember when Jesus sent us out by twos with power over the demons? How excited the people in the villages were to see us?"

"I loved seeing the demons run and the people cheer."

"I wish we could do that every day."

"Maybe we can," muses the third man.

"What do you mean?"

"Well, isn't Jesus always telling us to have more faith? Why not just ask him?"

In one unconscious second, each one has a vision of the future.

If I had more faith, just imagine the amazing things I would do!

When he hears about the difference I'm making, my father will be so proud of me!

I'll be <u>somebody</u>, not the apostle whose name no one remembers.

"Let's go tell the others!"

———

Later, wound up with anticipation, the twelve disciples barely listen to what Jesus is saying. "The very worst thing that can happen is if your behavior causes any of these vulnerable people to slip and slide away from God. Don't be the one who trips them up. Be the one who warns them about danger in the road so they can turn their lives around. And forgive them, no matter what they do, or how many times they do it."

Looking around the fidgety circle, Jesus wonders if they have a clue about how much responsibility he has just handed them. Or, he worries to himself, about how much more responsibility is barreling down the road toward them.

Seeing Jesus draw a breath to say something else, one of them blurts out, "Make our faith bigger!"

Smiling like proud children who have cleaned their rooms without being asked, the twelve wait for Jesus to say, "At last, you finally understand what's really important!" Not so very long ago, they heard Jesus muttering to himself, "How long do I have to put up with this faithless generation!" But this time he doesn't say, "Great, let's do it" the way they expect. He doesn't even smile at their request. Instead, in clipped tones, he answers them, "If you had faith as small as a mustard seed, you could get one of these mulberry trees to tear itself out by the roots and plant itself in the sea."

Confusion creases their foreheads and the twelve avoid each other's eyes.

Jesus stands up and walks alone toward the mulberry trees. He'd like to pull out his hair more than he'd like to pull out one of the trees. He smiles at his joke and begins to feel better.

A few months ago, the disciples' lack of faith was an issue, but that isn't the problem these days. The new concern is that the twelve are thinking of faith as a useful product and Jesus as their dealer. They'd like a Super-Sized Spectacular Faith, a faith that will give them the spiritual muscle they need to accomplish astonishing feats, with a spiritual high and an ego boost thrown in. They've begun thinking about faith as if it were their personal superpower. Their faith has gotten too big for its britches. Not unlike the faith of many today.

One variety of twenty-first century super-sized faith conveniently no longer even requires a belief in God. Simply fill your mind with the stuff you want, think positive thoughts about getting it, and the universe will send it your way. Want a Ferrari? Pin a picture of it to your bathroom mirror and be upbeat about it. The universe will sense all those positive vibes, and you'll get your car.

With a trendy Christian veneer, this sort of faith allows you to explain to people why they aren't being healed or why they can't find a job. In contrast, *your* business (or church) succeeds, *your* children go to Harvard and *you* have God figured out. Everyone is impressed by your results and spirituality. Your faith has put you at the top of the heap. You are a Christian Superhero.

A Czech priest named Tomás Halik believes super-sized faith is full of pitfalls.[2] Halik honed his understanding of God and faith during the persecutions of communism and has arrived at some startling conclusions. He proposes that when God feels cozy and manageable, our faith doesn't need to get any bigger, it needs to get much, much smaller. Instead of super-sized faith, Halik recommends we set our sights on a small stripped-down faith. A faith without the human add-ons that have made God out to be predictable and the good life one success after another. Halik suggests that genuine spiritual fruit more often than not comes from small seed-sized faith. The super-sized spectacular faith many people want, bears rotten fruit.

Know-it-all super-sized faith has no staying power when unintelligible suffering hits like a tsunami and sweeps you into a sea of impenetrable questions.

Super-sized faith can't help you absorb the inside-out mystery of the God whose modus operandi is to win by losing and grow by shrinking. Perhaps when super-sized faith begins to fade, even die, that's when faith in the God-Who-Really-Is can start to come into its own.

———

While the disciples are still standing there scuffing their toes in the dust, wondering why on earth they would want to tell a mulberry tree to pull itself up by the roots, Jesus comes back and tells them a story.

If he was here, telling his story to us, he might say, once there was a man who filled out his income tax form on April 10th. He filed electronically so it was totally legible, and he attached all the schedules and W-2s and forms he was supposed to include. He entered the correct routing number so the IRS could withdraw the amount due from his account. Once he inserted his e-signature, and pressed <u>send</u>, he gave a sigh of relief and poured himself a drink. He didn't sit by the phone waiting for a grateful call from the IRS. He didn't peek into his mailbox every day to see if the thank-you note from the President's office had arrived yet. He acted like the citizen he was, obeying the law and paying his taxes, even though half the time he wasn't at all pleased with how his money was being spent. He just did what he thought every American ought to do and was expected to do. He was faithful to his responsibility as a citizen.

The disciples say to Jesus, give us more faith, so Jesus tells them a story that says *live a faithful life*. Faith is most spectacular, not when it is healing, casting out demons or planting big churches, but when it is being loyal to what Jesus said was important. So incredibly loyal, in fact, that a person full of faith actually pays attention to other people's spiritual and material well-being and continuously forgives them when they screw up.

Sometimes, I have wished for a big faith that would make all my troubles go away. Being successful and admired would be useful too. Faith didn't work like that for Peter or Paul or for the Old Testament prophets. It especially didn't work that way for Jesus. Instead, faith made them faithful, able to stick with

God when life felt grungy and when nothing made sense. Or maybe their faithfulness gave them faith, ability to sense God sticking with them in spite of their troubles. Or maybe both/and.

Little faith isn't dazzling or spectacular. It doesn't feed your ego or make you a legendary superhero. It happens one foot in front of another, day by day and year by year. Eventually, without you even noticing, the landscape begins to change wherever you are. And one day maybe you'll stop to wonder whatever happened to that mulberry tree.

In a world that shouts, "supersize me," big turns out to be very, very small.

Journaling Starter

Has your faith been growing or shrinking? Or both? What sort of faith appeals to you right now?

How would viewing faith as loyalty to God impact your spiritual life?

The woman was Greek,
Syro-Phoenician by birth.
She asked him to cure her daughter.

Mark 7:26 (The Message)

NINE

Dog Days

My brother and I bickered about everything when we were children. One day my mother brought home a jumbo sized piece of chocolate cake from the bakery near her office. This had happened before and it always ended in a fight about who would get the larger half. This time, my mother offered us the treat and told us that one of us would slice the cake, but the other one would choose the first piece. When they were passing out spatial ability my brother received his share plus all of mine, so I was happy to let him cut, and even more happily looked forward to choosing the larger slice. I patiently stood aside while my brother spent five minutes eyeballing the cake and aiming the knife at the precise center of the gooey chocolate tower. Carefully wielding the knife, he smiled in satisfaction when the deed was done. I minutely examined each slice, but they were completely, precisely equal. We both enjoyed our cake that day. And so did our mother.

In the world of psychology this is called a zero sum game. That means there is a limited amount to go around—so if you get some, I'll get that much less. For people in the first century Mediterranean world, it wasn't a game. Everything was zero sum. Everything.

———

The middle-aged mother from Tyre[3] trudged up the steep path, which had been described to her, and nervously wondered if it had been right to leave her cart and apprehensive driver at the edge of this unfamiliar neighborhood. Local women cast hostile looks at her Greek style of dress, probably thinking they knew what kind of woman she was.

She sighed bleakly. Would a Master of virtue, a servant of God, attend to a shameless Greek matron alone in the streets? It did not seem very likely. But to drive up like condescending aristocrat seemed even more offensive.

Pausing on the rocky street, she pressed a sleeve to her welling eyes. She tried to force her mind to recall when her daughter Kalliope had stopped speaking. The memory was not there.

All she knew for sure was that the nightmare had begun during the rising of Sirius, the Dog Star.

She could recollect standing in the atrium of her summer villa. She had just finished directing the foreman to have their people begin harvesting the snails for brewing imperial dye. Her husband would not want it delayed. Mid-summer was the time of year it was always done, and production of Tyrian royal purple depended on it. At any rate, the ship was only overdue by a few days. It made no sense to wait until her husband and sons were home. Thinking of them, she had smiled a little as she watched an unexpected figure approaching the entrance to the villa. The ship's owner.

A lifetime ago.

Had weeks passed? Months? She did not know. Everything after the Accident remained shadowed. The only thing her mind was willing to release from that terrible time was a memory of summoning the doctor from Alexandria for Kalliope. The day the doctor finally arrived, he observed the mute girl, shook his head, and recommended hot baths and a sacrifice to Asclepius, the Greek god of healing. Then he sailed back to Alexandria, along with his hefty fee. Soon after he left, Kalliope gashed her arms with thorns from the bushes in the garden until her flesh wept blood.

Love for Kalliope had kept her alive, though living meant dragging her body and darkened mind through meaningless time and space. To survive, she dammed up thoughts of the past, or the present, or the bitter future. Yet quite strangely, one morning, as she awoke, something from before the accident seeped through. The image of a dinner guest who told tales about Tyrian men encountering a healer in the Galilee.

———

Months later, along a dusty road, somewhere in Galilee, men whisper to each other. "I don't see why we have to go way up there to get away from the crowds."

"It's the last place I would have chosen."

"Those Tyrians are just Syrian flunkies. They're all the same."

"They're vultures. They buy up all the grain in Galilee and leave us nothing."

"They'll be lining up to destroy us if they ever get another chance."

Suddenly aware of another man who wasn't there before, the others wonder how much he's heard. But all Jesus says is "Let's go."

Jesus sighs, adjusts the pack on his shoulders, and then trots past the lagging disciples. Running alone, he thinks long and hard about the tightrope he's trying to walk, cherishing the Jews on one hand and conveying his compassion for the rest of the world on the other. Months ago he sent the disciples out in pairs to preach to people of the countryside. He had instructed them not to mix with gentiles or Samaritans, but to interact only with fellow Jews. It was the right decision…but the disciples have understood it all wrong.

One thing that every Jew living under Roman rule could agree on (and they couldn't agree on much) was that Israel had an exclusive relationship with God. They were Chosen—all the way back to Abraham. So even though the Jews didn't have the land, the money, or the power, the Jews had God. Any hint that this state of affairs might start shifting to the *gentiles'* favor made most of them go ballistic. One time, back in Nazareth, Jesus had reminded the townspeople that hundreds of years ago some despised foreigners in Sidon and Syria had received God's help rather than the folks back home. The people in the pews just about lynched him.

People figured that anything Jesus might do for a bunch of godless foreigners (who had tried to obliterate them on more than one occasion) meant there would be that much less Jesus could do for them. There was no way red-blooded Galileans were going to let *that* happen. Did looking out for number one contradict what the Prophets and Writings taught about God's compassion for the nations? Did it contradict what Jesus had already said to them? Or what he'd done? Sure it did, but like us, they were too wrapped up in their own way of thinking and bitter experiences to notice.

But Jesus noticed. The lynch mob was probably his first clue. Anyway, he understood that sometimes a person can have all the best information, but still be a long hard road away from the kind of knowing that seeps down into your soul.

So Jesus had decided to take the disciples to Tyre. Why would he go on vacation in a place reviled by Jews? Certainly not because he needed to let people know how much he despised non-Jews. (The Pharisees did a better job of that by avoiding gentiles altogether!) True, he wanted a rest. But anyone with a bigoted aversion to gentiles would have ferreted out an undiscovered retreat center in rural Galilee. Anything, rather than go walkabout in Tyre.

Jesus deliberately chose Tyre, at least partly, so he could begin to show the disciples some of the tangled assumptions they held about anyone who was "not one of us"—and, more importantly, the tangled assumptions they held about God.

A distraught woman throws herself onto the ground in front of a small group of startled men. Laboring over each word, she chokes out, "Have mercy on me Master. I beg you. My daughter. She doesn't talk. She cuts herself. An unclean spirit tortures her. Please help me. Please." Sobbing in misery and humiliation, the woman covers her face and gasps for air.

Jesus waits. He waits for the woman to collect herself. He waits to see what the disciples might do. He waits.

After a long pause, one of the twelve doles out some advice. "Just send her away. We came here to rest and spend important time together, not to get sidetracked by some demented foreigner. Since we're here, at least let's have some peace."

With a penetrating look at his companions, Jesus softly turns to the woman now catching her breath. He says out loud what he's certain his disciples are thinking. "I was sent to take care of the children of Israel, not snatch bread out of their mouths and toss it to scavenging dogs. Everyone knows there is not enough to go around."

Hearing Jesus' voice, the woman's heart begins to pound. He's not sending her away empty-handed, at least not yet. Perhaps there's hope. But how strange. Especially for a Jewish holy man. Men with reputations to uphold do not strike up conversations with strange women on the sidewalk.

But then, every story about him has been unexpected. What was it the servant she sent to Galilee reported about him? "Jesus teaches that God showers the rain and shines the sun on everyone. He said God loves even the people who don't recognize him, and that God knows how to give good gifts. I heard that one time Jesus even healed a Roman centurion's slave."

That was the Jesus she had come hoping to find. Pushing all her chips to the middle of the table, she quietly wagers, "Yes, Master, of course you must care for your own needy people. The Jews are privileged by God. But there is more than enough of God to go around. He doesn't run out of good gifts. The dogs under the table will eat the crumbs that fall while the children are fed. There is plenty for everyone."

Speechless, the twelve gape at her while Jesus grins. *This will give them something to chew over. In more ways than one! What a remarkable person.*

"Woman, you have put your finger on it! Go home unashamed to your daughter. She is well, and lucky to have a mother willing to stake everything on the big-heartedness of God.

And now gentlemen, if you'll pack our gear, we're going further on…to Sidon."

It was time for some big slices of chocolate cake, all around.

Journaling Starter

Is there a person or group of people whom you feel God ought to shun? Do you ever feel that God is shunning you, or that he can't spare the time to listen to you? What relationships or experiences (especially from your childhood) might have pointed you toward a zero sum view of God?

But he was in the stern, asleep on the cushion;
and they woke him up and said to him,
"Teacher, do you not care that we are perishing?"

Mark 4:38

TEN

Leaving the Shore Line

I grew up in Colorado, about a thousand miles from the nearest beach. My first boat ride, at age nine, was across smooth and sunny Lake Michigan while vacationing with my family. I loved the feel of the air and the sound of the waves. I didn't lay eyes on an ocean until I was twenty-one, but it didn't matter. I knew I loved the water. Safely, from a distance.

The Galileans were from landlocked territory too. They lived and fished by the shore of a sixty-five square mile lake, and as far as they were concerned only a crazy person would go boating on anything larger. The sudden violent windstorms on the Sea of Galilee confirmed their opinion that demons haunted open waters and stirred up the waves. Let the Gentiles risk their lives sailing the Mediterranean, but not them, no sir. The Sea of Galilee was bad enough. Find yourself In the middle of the Sea of Galilee during one of those storms, and God would be your only hope.

Just a year ago, four Galilean cousins had abandoned their family fishing business in order to follow Jesus. One of their dads must have finally calmed down about the blow to the family economy, because he let them borrow one of the fishing boats to ferry Jesus back and forth to his teaching engagements. That afternoon, Jesus had even used the boat as a makeshift pulpit, deciding it was safer to sit in the boat to teach than to risk being pushed into the water by the crowd.

As the sun set, Jesus sent the people home, and told the disciples to sail for the big harbor on the gentile side of the lake, while he took a nap. They felt a cold wind sweeping down the hills, the first hint of a coming storm, but nobody mentioned it. They could see Jesus needed a break. And they were sure they could beat the weather.

About an hour later, out in the middle of the lake, the wind exploded. The night sky turned completely dark. Ten-foot waves blocked out the moon and crashed into the little fishing boat. If they took a breaking wave over the side of the boat, the boat would flip, and down they would all go, straight to the bottom.

The disciples do what any self-reliant, strong men do when confronted with life-threatening danger. They shriek, "We're all gonna die!!"

As the shrieking tapers off, they realize Jesus isn't there screaming along with them. They decide somebody better go and find him. (My guess is they sent Peter; he always liked telling Jesus what to do.) They don't expect Jesus to do anything much; they just want him to be scared with them and keep them company while they drown.

———

Peter doubles up against the wind and drags himself hand over hand along the starboard rails. He can't see a thing in the pitch black, but he knows every inch of his boat, and he senses he is nearing the stern. Just then, he trips over the edge of a sandbag and falls to his knees. He can barely make out the figure of Jesus, tucked under the aft deck, sound asleep on top of the sandbag. Relief floods him, instantly followed by fury.

Peter shakes Jesus—hard—and then shouts over the howling wind, "Don't you even care that we are out here dying! You aren't seasick, you aren't overboard, you're not even scared! We need you to come and be with us, not sleep until we're all dead!" Jesus stretches like he's about to roll over and go back to his nap. "If he tries that," Peter swears to himself, "I'll throw Jesus overboard, storm or no storm!" But Jesus grunts, stands up, and hollers like a drill sergeant at the storm, "Stop it! Settle down!"

Instantly, the wind goes weak as a breeze and, instead of surging over the decks, the lake waters begin to lap at the hull. The moon lights up the sky, but the disciples don't shout or cheer. In fact, they can't move. They can't utter a sound.

That's when Jesus raises a single eyebrow and calmly asks, "You still don't know what to believe, do you? What are you afraid of? *Really?*"

Then he stretches out on the deck and looks at the stars.

———

On a hot summer night in old town Albuquerque, the stars were just beginning to twinkle as my grandfather and I reached the end of the sidewalk. Without warning, swooping, spraying fountains sprang out of the patio in front of us, while multi-colored lights turned them into rainbows. The whooshing sound of the splashing water, the feel of the cool mist on my skin, and the pastel colors shimmering on the white foam filled me with peace and wonder. I was from a small town in the west and had never seen anything so beautiful.

For once, my impatient family wasn't hurrying me along. It was just my grandfather, who was willing to let me soak in the experience for as long as I wanted. He didn't say a word, just waited and smiled at my pleasure. I don't know how long we stood there, but long enough to last my lifetime. Fountains of all kinds still transport me to the same lovely interior place, and a lighted fountain brings tears to my eyes.

Those lighted fountains of Albuquerque, New Mexico, were my first experience of transcendence, though I did not know that word until decades had passed.

Even for a little girl or an old man, sometimes the One-Who-Is raises the hem of the curtain that separates this world from the one beyond. Then an unseen presence radiates over and around us. Time as we know it disappears and another kind of time takes its place. The sun rises and reaches the top of the sky, but it feels as if only a single hour has passed. Or the clock ticks off one-hundred seconds, but the moment swells to the size of eternity. When the uncanny touches us, we may step back in apprehension. Yet in our trepidation, a yearning pulls us nearer. Spellbound, men and women find their eyes filling with overwhelming emotion. During such encounters, we may even find ourselves unable to speak or move.

Once we have experienced the transcendent One-Who-Is, we long to experience more, but we cannot manipulate the enchanted moment to come again. It will not come on our schedule and it will not come by our will. That's how we know it is God.

Simon skips a stone across the water, watching it bounce along the waves. His friend Matthew gazes down the shoreline.

"Were you close enough to hear him, Matthew? When he ordered the storm to stop blowing?"

"Yes. No. I don't know. It seems like I heard him, but I couldn't have, not from the other end of the boat. Not in that wind."

"When the wind stopped, I went weak as a kitten. Scared as one, too."

"I was too. But I still wanted it to go on forever."

"He barked out orders to the water and wind. Who or What does something like that?"

Simon's thumb and fingers squeeze his temples, as if to knead thoughts that refuse to take shape. Eyes closed, his words push out in a whisper. "I saw a fire once when I was a kid. A couple of houses burned down. It was so terrible and powerful and yet so beautiful all at the same time."

"Like last night."

After another silence Matthew squints toward the sunshine twinkling across the water and murmurs, "There are times when the light vanishes behind darkening clouds; then comes the wind, sweeping them away, and brightness spreads from the north. God is clothed in fearful splendor."[4]

"What's that from?"

The book of Job."

"Poor old Job. So much misery. And God never even answered his questions."

"I know...do you suppose maybe he at least ended up with different questions?"

Yes. Different questions. When I was a boy all my questions were about fishing. Always I was asking where do the fish hide, how do I cast the net, steer the boat, hoist the sail? My father drilled those things into me before I ever left the shallows. The day he finally let me sail away from land, I thought I was a real fisher at last. What did I know then? Not much. It takes a lifetime to know the sea, know the fish. Up until last night, I thought I knew Jesus. I haven't even left the shore line.

Journaling Starter

What memories or experiences of wonder or the uncanny have stayed with you?

Have you ever encountered God in a way you didn't expect or control?

And the Spirit immediately drove Jesus
out into the wilderness.
He was in the wilderness forty days,
tempted by Satan.

Mark 1:12–13

ELEVEN

Scrub Brush and Scorpions

I am not a wilderness lover. This is a terrible admission for a Colorado native! My friends know I am not good at dirt, creeping things, or hard sleeping surfaces. The closest I can come to loving the wilderness is in a cabin with a dishwasher, doors that lock, and good plumbing. Other people are crazy about the wilderness and go camping every chance they get. They find the scenery breathtaking, the air invigorating, and the peace untouchable. Wilderness cuts both ways. And so it is throughout the Bible. Paradoxically, wilderness is a place of scarcity and danger and evil, but also a place of guidance and transformation and seeing God.

Jesus, the carpenter, travelled down to the Jordan River where his cousin John was baptizing people. His reasons for going were not like those of his friends and neighbors. He wasn't motivated by guilt, curiosity or even the wish to find God. Instead, Jesus was propelled by love for God, as he had been every day of his life. As he pictured the whole nation gathering at the river to repent, he choked up. These desperate people were the very ones he hoped to restore to God. Meeting them, with John, down at the Jordan felt like the right thing to do.

So down to the river he went, and asked John to plunge him under the water. He came up dripping, and caught sight of the Holy Spirit soaring towards him like a dove. A voice from heaven thundered that he was much loved, and the Father was proud of him. Jesus hadn't come to the river expecting any of this. Even for Jesus, visible and audible displays of God's devotion did not happen every day. In fact, this was a first.

Basking in the glow of being treasured and affirmed, feeling a greater weight of destiny and spiritual strength than ever before, Jesus might have sensed he was at a turning point. Maybe he started making plans about what he wanted to do next. Head home and put his affairs in order. Finish that carpentry job. Tell his mom what was up. Only his life doesn't work the way he expects. The very same Spirit who only a moment ago filled him up with blessing, immediately drives him out, deep into the wilderness, toward danger, temptation, and terror.

He doesn't even get a chance to grab a blanket.

Those first lonely days and nights in the wilderness, he had time on his hands to do some hard thinking. That is, when he wasn't fighting off hyenas with a stick. How would this wilderness thing play out? Would God show up and rescue him soon? Would there be food from heaven? Water? How about GPS?

The wilderness was an in-between place for Jesus. He had left his role as the carpenter from Nazareth but hadn't taken up a new way of life as wandering Rabbi. It was one thing to be God's son back in Nazareth, out of harm's way, living the life everyone expected him to live. But he wasn't there now and might never go back. God had named him his Beloved Son at his baptism, but what did that actually mean here in the wilderness, when he was vulnerable and in danger? What could God be thinking, leaving him alone—and when would it be over? What was the point of all this delay?

He had plenty of time to wonder what God's love means when nothing is safe or predictable, and God isn't getting you out of there and back home nearly so soon as you hoped he would. Plenty of time for mulling over his predicament. Plenty of time for questions. Plenty of time for everything except answers.

Being alone in a wilderness for a week, without a tent or any gear, is going to be a grim camping trip, no matter how much of an outdoors guy you are. It's going to jolt you out of the ordinary, use up all your energy and it's going to take super concentration not to make stupid mistakes. Make it more than a couple of weeks, and now we are talking life or death.

And then just when you reach the end of your rope, when whatever resources you have scrounged together have totally run out, when you feel like you haven't got any strength, or wit, or determination left, here comes Satan. He's raising even more disturbing and unsettling possibilities.

"So what if God said you are his son and he loves you. What does that <u>mean</u> anyway? Words are cheap. Look around. Who's taking care of you? No one, that's who. Why wait on God, when he isn't doing anything for you? You're the miracle man; why not use your gifts to take care of yourself?"

"And, on top of that, here you are doing exactly what God told you to do, and what are you getting out of it? Nothing, that's what. You've done what he asked you to do, but what is he doing for <u>you</u>? Where is he? Why keep on waiting? Why not force God's hand and bring this to a head. Jump off this tower and <u>make</u> God show up."

"In fact, why not get the whole thing over with right now," says Satan. "I can give you everything God can, power and triumph and success, and I'll do it right now without all this misery, trouble and pointless waiting around—and without that cross that you know is coming your way. Turn your back on God, bow down to me, and we've got a deal."

———

We have no idea how long these questions swirled around in Jesus' head. We don't know how much time went by before he was ready to reply. He had to dig down deep when it seemed like God had gone missing, when what he thought he knew about God, what he thought he knew about himself, started feeling like it might be up for grabs.

Finally, when all his old familiar, comfortable ways of engaging God were no longer enough for him, Jesus grew to perceive the sheer silence of God as Presence. After a long, long time, through the thick cloud of unknowing that is the plight of humanity, he came to sense even deeper realities. The wilderness became a chrysalis for Jesus, strengthening his wisdom and grounding in God, preparing him to take up his public role as Suffering Servant and Christ, tempering him like steel for the even harder journey to the cross that lay ahead.

In the wilderness, Jesus found that his life with God did not depend on personal comfort. He knew in the depths of his soul that serving his own needs wasn't the point. When Satan challenged him to turn stones into bread, Jesus did not simply recite a suitable Bible verse. He had learned in the trenches that he could feast on God. "One does not live by bread alone"[5] had become his own wisdom.

When Satan prodded Jesus to throw himself off the temple to make God show up, Jesus didn't need to prove, to himself or to anyone, that God was present. Jesus was ready to bank on the fact that his relationship with God was not a business deal—not a transaction where 'I do something for you, you do something for me.' He could say "Do not put the Lord your God to the test"[6] because he had absorbed down to his bones the reality that he was a Son, not a client or customer. In the midst of emptiness Jesus became sensitive to a different sort of abundance—an abundance of love and care, not reluctantly doled out by God in pieces, but poured out in showers.

If Jesus had any traces of human yearning for status and admiration, the wilderness stripped it all away. The wilderness etched into his soul what really mattered. Though his destiny was to launch and lead the reign of God, power and prestige did not intrigue him. Jesus had his heart set on the healing of the world, the redemption of the cosmos. When Satan offered to give him the kingdoms of the world, Jesus replied "Worship the Lord your God and serve him alone."[7] This was far more than a rule to follow. It was the paradigm in which he moved, the story out of which he lived.

Paradoxically, the difficulties and strivings of the wilderness left Jesus stronger, not weaker, and more resolute in his self-awareness and devotion to God. In the end, it was not Jesus the carpenter from Nazareth who emerged out of the wilderness, full of the Holy Spirit. It was Jesus the Messiah, the Anointed One.

Journaling Starter

Have you ever asked yourself any of the sorts of questions Satan asked Jesus? If so, what did you think and feel about yourself? About God?

Has an event or experience ever transformed your sense of who you are? or made you stronger in who you are?

We never really know enough
until we recognize that
God alone knows it all.

1 Corinthians 8:3 (The Message)

TWELVE

Ducks or Rabbits

Jesus was formed by his arduous experience in the wilderness, so we should not be too proud, or too surprised, when life puts us there. Of course, seasons of spiritual disorientation remain harrowing and unwanted. But they have the potential to open our eyes to richer images of God than we have seen so far. This was Jesus' hope for the people he encountered during his lifetime, and it is his hope for us.

Ironically, our ability to receive more wisdom about God, and about our own souls, often hinges on the muddling up of our old understanding. It is a bit like what happens when you stare at an optical illusion (or at least what happens when *I* stare at one). Is it a vase or two faces? Is it a duck or a rabbit? My brain does the best it can, but I usually have a terrible time seeing anything more than I saw in the first instant. I shake my head, blink my eyes, and squint, in the hope that I can scramble my brain and help it see more than it expected. Eventually, my brain spots the vase, and the more complex reality, that was there all the time. In a similar way, spiritual disorientation shakes us loose from the flawed suppositions and superficial reasoning that are no longer equal to the task at hand. Though the process is unnerving, disorientation increases our potential to discover and embrace qualities of God that have been hiding in plain sight.

When I was about thirty years old, my doctor diagnosed me with countless food sensitivities and placed me on a highly restricted diet. If I risked eating a morsel of Communion bread, muscle pain would send me home before the church service ended. I had no energy, couldn't work, and was unable to participate in the ministry I loved. I wanted to contribute to God's work, and wondered why God wouldn't let me do that.

It didn't make sense and I was often discouraged and frustrated. But if there was a way through, I was determined to find it.

Five years later, I had learned to work around my illness. I calculated that a few healthy hours every week would be enough for me to manage life as a part-time seminary student. I loved my classes and hoped to teach after graduation. I could feel myself coming back to life. Surely the storm was over and the good life had begun.

Then, without warning, like a flash flood after a downpour, financial hardship surged over my plans. The house was lost, money was owed, and my stipend was too small to help pay the bills. Devastated, I relinquished my scholarship and dropped out of graduate school, without hope of ever returning. I survived, but my dreams had been swept away.

Not long afterwards, I found myself sitting alone in a church pew, vacantly staring at a wooden post. It must be that God did not want me anymore. I couldn't imagine a way to be who I wanted to be, or even a way to be who I used to be. Unknowing stretched as far as my eye could see.

―――

Whenever an upside-down, nothing-makes-sense-anymore experience strands you in a disorienting wasteland, it may seem that white-knuckle survival is all that is possible. But there is another option. This option won't get you out of the wasteland, it won't make your pain go away, and it won't give you three easy steps to anything. But it will give you resilience while you are discovering your path by walking it. Resilience and well-being in a season of confusion will mean holding onto God, and your confusion about him, all at the same time. It will mean paying attention to the present reality of your soul, no matter what you might discover there.[8]

To begin, I suggest you to go to a restful spot where you won't be interrupted. Sit or lie down. Slowly breathe in and out and unwind. Become aware of your body in space and time. Begin to allow yourself to feel what you feel, as you feel it. Brave the sensations that bubble to the surface, rather than pressing them back down. If you have nothing to say, or if what you sense is emptiness, let yourself be speechless and empty. Don't run away. Be still, and breathe in-and-out the silence and nothingness. If your soul releases anger, fear or sadness, pour it out, straight to God, out loud or on paper. When your own words fail you, consider the words of the Psalms.

Holding on to God means pouring out your soul before him. But holding onto God also means making the most of ordinary moments. It means letting yourself notice, then experience down to your toes, any trace of the beautiful and good in and around you. Even in the wilderness there are hints of color and life! Slow down to sniff a honeysuckle, sit by a melodious wind chime, or gaze at the oranges and pinks of the setting sun. Consciously create something—write or paint or cook. Watch for someone to help who can't return the favor. Practicing this way of being yourself with God, and in the world, will nourish your soul. It will keep you close to the ground and safe from flying debris when the pillars that have buttressed your life begin to shake.

The wilderness of unknowing is a fierce and wild place, and stretches further than we think we can bear. Yet if we attend to God and our souls in the midst of it, we find a mysterious well-being there. Jesus understood this. After his wilderness ordeal ended, he often returned alone to the wilderness to pray and listen. You would think scrub brush and scorpions would be the last things Jesus would ever want to see again. Yet Jesus had a keen awareness that the wilderness is a place where God lingers with his people.

Twenty-five years have passed since I sat bewildered in the church pew staring at a post. Though subsequent events in my life have been more tragic, none of them have proved as baffling. Like all wilderness experiences, the disorientation I experienced was incredibly demanding. At the same time, it accomplished a life-giving paradigm shift. I came to see and sense that God uses the unknowing of terrible experiences to transform us. Though God recycles, reuses, and repurposes all the garbage and confusion of life, this does not mean he orchestrates tragedy and harm. He is the author of life and the sworn enemy of physical and spiritual death. God is on our side, suffering and weeping with us.

These perceptions of God have transformed my inner world, but sometimes I still wish life would make logical sense! This appears to be delusional, because, seen from the outside, my life makes less sense than ever. But whether life makes sense or not, God is here and he is bigger than I used to see, and that is better than rational answers.

I have experienced many seasons of disorientation over my lifetime. After each one, I have developed a greater ability to embrace paradox and mystery and to love God for himself alone. I have learned that seasons of disorientation do not need to deteriorate into spiritual defects. They can become sacred doorways of transformation. Though disorientation is never what I want, and always involves a long, long wait, each coke bottle that falls from the sky leads me to a more breath-taking God.

Welcome to confusion.

Journaling Starter

What seasons of unknowing have you had so far? Have you ever received anything worthwhile from a season of unknowing? If you are in the middle of a season of confusion now, what is it like for you?

Having Doubts about Doubting?

Does the Bible teach that uncertainty and questions are the opposite of faith? Here are a few Biblical selections to help you consider if, or when, the Bible is opposed to confusion.

For God is not the author of confusion but of peace.

1 Corinthians 14:33 (KJV)

The Apostle Paul wrote a letter to the church in Corinth after hearing how disorderly and divisive their meetings had become. He gave the church some guidelines for reducing chaos without quenching the Holy Spirit.

When Paul wrote that "God is not the author of confusion but of peace" he was worried about commotion in public worship. He wasn't worried that people had questions; he was worried about the wild way they asked those questions. People were talking and shouting over each other. The word confusion in this text is from a Greek word that is translated elsewhere as "disorder," "unruliness" or "dissension" and even sometimes as "riots." Attending church in Corinth must have been a rowdy experience!

This verse does not refer to anyone's spiritual or psychological confusion. It refers to community behaviors that actually distract people from the worship of God. Worship sparked by the Holy Spirit and pleasing to God doesn't look like a mob scene.[9]

**I know your works; you are neither cold nor hot.
I wish that you were either cold or hot.
So, because you are lukewarm,
and neither cold nor hot,
I am about to spit you out of my mouth.**

Revelation 3:15–16

A generation or two after Jesus' death and resurrection, John the Seer, wrote down Christ's directives for seven churches in Asia Minor. The Risen Christ said to John, "Tell Laodicea they are so lukewarm they make me want to vomit."

This text is often quoted to push those with questions to become more convinced about their faith. Setting aside the issue of whether a good scare can shake people out of uncertainty, this interpretation raises some perplexing questions. Wouldn't you think Christ would reject stone-cold followers as well as lukewarm ones? Does this text really mean that the church in Laodicea was wavering in its faith? Could this text possibly mean something else?

Lutheran scholar Craig Koester believes this text reveals that Christ is looking for followers who *contrast with their surroundings.* No one goes to a restaurant and orders a lukewarm soda or tepid coffee. Christ wants hot or cold disciples the same way people want a cold drink on a hot day and a hot drink on a cold day.

The church in Laodicea was economically wealthy and complacent (Rev 3:17), just like the pagan city where it was located. The church was so comfortable that it blended right in with local values and customs. It was no different than the surrounding society.[10] Its fatal flaw was self-absorption and marriage to the status quo. And the worst of it was that the church was completely oblivious to its spiritual poverty. Some honest doubt and engagement would have been a big improvement over the blind complacency of the church in Laodicea.

> **But ask in faith, never doubting…for the doubter, being double-minded and unstable in every way, must not expect to receive anything from the Lord.**
>
> James 1:6–9

Belief, experience, and ethical integrity are three vital aspects of the Christian life. But right from the beginning, the church had to work at keeping all three components in play. Each era has tended to over or under-emphasize one or more of them. For example, during our century, a new emphasis on experience has remedied its earlier neglect. However, by refocusing on spiritual encounters, we may have diminished the importance of doctrine and virtue.

In the early decades of Christianity, James, a leader of the church in Jerusalem, was worried that

Christians were letting integrity take a back seat to belief. He wrote to warn first century followers of Christ that genuine faith requires worthy behavior, not simply belief. Contemporary people, steeped in an understanding of faith as personal experience, can easily misjudge James' concerns.

When early twenty-first century people hear the word doubt, they typically visualize an inner psychological feeling or experience of "uncertainty or questioning."[11] Presbyterian scholar Dan G. McCartney insists that this is not consistent with James' intent. He argues that in James' letter "'doubt'…is best understood as the wavering of allegiance…not the failure to expunge uncertainty."[12]

Anyone reading the book of James straight through will notice how James encourages his readers to complete their faith through what they do. He has little, if any, interest in what they feel or even think. James identifies certain actions that correspond to Christian values as well as other actions that do not: Since you have faith, do works. Since you bless our Lord and Father, don't curse those made in God's image. There are many analogies like this scattered throughout the five chapters. James continually emphasizes his concern for his reader's conduct, but demonstrates no interest in their inner psychological state. McCartney argues that the doubt James condemns is "a divided loyalty," a concept that "can be traced back to...Jesus, who... point[ed] out that no one can serve two masters."[13]

Instead of commending emotional certainty, James is calling his readers to match their conduct to their spiritual convictions. His zeal for spiritual fidelity is underlined by his concluding exhortation, "Adulterers! Do you not know that friendship with the world is enmity with God?" (James 4:4). When James says "do not doubt," he is not concerned about psychological turmoil. He is focused instead on confronting spiritual infidelity and the need for Christians to live with integrity.

**Now faith is the assurance of things hoped for,
the conviction of things not seen.**

Hebrews 11:1

This is a difficult verse to understand because it contains two concepts for which English has no simple equivalents. The author/preacher of Hebrews explains that faith is *hypostasis,* or an underlying reality. Second, faith is *elencho,* a term Greek philosophers used for the Socratic questioning that engages learners in self-examination. The aim of this self-examination was to help people discover the flaws in their thinking, refine their ideas, and own the truth for themselves.[14]

Some English translations of Hebrews 11:1 come close to capturing the original meaning of the verse. John Wycliffe's translation (from about 1380 A.D.) reads, "But faith is the substance of things that are to be hoped, and an argument of things not appearing."[15] Wycliffe selected the English word "substance" to indicate the essential core or underlying reality. His word "argument" alludes to the Socratic dialogue which empowers people to own the truth for themselves. Writing six hundred years after Wycliffe, Eugene

Peterson translated this verse as, "The fundamental fact of existence is that this trust in God, this faith, is the firm foundation under everything that makes life worth living. It's our handle on what we can't see."[16] This rendering of the text provides helpful insight to contemporary readers.

Over the past fifty years, Hebrews 11:1 has often been translated using words like "assurance" or "conviction" or even "certainty". Though not invalid, translations like these may inadvertently imply that faith is a subjective intellectual, or even emotional, experience. To some non-specialists, these word choices may even suggest that anyone less than totally convicted, assured, and certain lacks adequate faith. But the original language of this verse makes it clear that faith is not a subjective thought or feeling. Faith stands on what actually exists. Faith allows us to take in the unseen realities for ourselves. New Testament scholar and former Benedictine monk, Luke Timothy Johnson, explains that because faith "connects to something real,"[17] it is the way we actually participate in the life and nature of God.

Thus, faith is personal and authentic but it is not subjective. Faith is not a psychological state but an objective reality. As the author of Hebrews goes on to demonstrate in chapter eleven, faith is not measured by emotion, but by actions of fidelity, the way a life is lived for God.

Journaling Starter

Are uncertainties and questions the opposite of faith?
What does it mean to have faith?

Wrestling with God's Incomprehensibility: A Biblical Pedigree

Wrestling with God's incomprehensibility leads us on journeys towards a bigger God. Here are examples of biblical wrestlers whose questions and confusion ultimately drew them more deeply into God's presence.

Job: You have turned cruel to me; with the might of your hand you persecute me. You lift me up on the wind, you make me ride on it, and you toss me about in the roar of the storm. I know that you will bring me to death, and to the house appointed for all living (Job 30:21–23).

The Psalmist (about twenty-five per cent of the psalms express confusion or questions about God.): I am so troubled that I cannot speak. Has God forgotten to be gracious? Has he in anger shut up his compassion? (Psalm 77:4, 9).

Jeremiah: You will be in the right, O LORD, when I lay charges against you; but let me put my case to you. Why does the way of the guilty prosper? Why do all who are treacherous thrive? (Jeremiah 12:1).

Habakkuk: O LORD, how long shall I cry for help and you will not listen? Or cry to you "Violence!" and you will not save? Why do you make me see wrongdoing and look at trouble? (Habakkuk 1:2–3).

John the Baptist: When John heard in prison what the Messiah was doing, he sent word by his disciples and said to him, "Are you the one who is to come, or are we to wait for another?" (Matthew 11:2–3).

Mary: And [Gabriel] came to [Mary] and said, "Greetings, favored one! The Lord is with you." But she was much perplexed by his words and pondered what sort of greeting this might be (Luke 1:28–29). And now, you will conceive in your womb and bear a son, and you will name him Jesus. ...Mary said to the angel, "How can this be, since I am a virgin?" (Luke 1:31, 34).

Peter: Now while Peter was greatly puzzled about what to make of the vision that he had seen, suddenly the men sent by Cornelius appeared (Acts 10:17).

Paul: We are afflicted in every way, but not crushed; perplexed, but not driven to despair (2 Corinthians 4:8).

Notes

One

The Gods Must be Crazy

1. Directed by Jamie Uys. (1980, Ster Kinekor Pictures). The exclamation point in !Kung is the standard notation for a click sound found in some African languages.

Eight

Small is the New Big: The Twelve

2. My understanding of "mustard-seed faith" is indebted to the stimulating thoughts of Tomás Halik on the subject. Tomás Halik, *Night of the Confessor: Christian Faith in an Age of Uncertainty* (New York: Doubleday Religion, 2012), 17–33.

Nine

Dog Days: The Syrophoenician Woman

3. I recommend Kenneth E. Bailey's chapter on the Syrophoenician woman in his book *Jesus Through Middle Eastern Eyes* (Downers Grove: InterVarsity Press, 2008), 217–226.

Ten

Leaving the Shore Line: Simon

4. Job 37:21–22 excerpted from *The New Jerusalem Bible.*

Eleven

Scrub Brush and Scorpions: Jesus

5. Deuteronomy 8:3.
6. Deuteronomy 6:16.
7. Deuteronomy 8:19.

Twelve

Ducks or Rabbits: All of Us

8. Trauma victims should not attempt this without the support of a qualified therapist. Lack of feeling after a shock or trauma is a natural protective cocoon which must be wisely and gently unwrapped.

Postscript

Having Doubts about Doubting?

9. David E. Garland, *1 Corinthians* (Grand Rapids: Baker Academic, 2003), 664.
10. Craig R. Koester, "The Message to Laodicea and the Problem of Its Local Context: A Study of the Imagery in Rev 3.14–22," *New Testament Studies* 49, no. 3 (July 2003): 409, 415.
11. Dan G. McCartney, *James,* (Grand Rapids: Baker Academic, 2009), 91.
12. Ibid, 90, n. 14.
13. Ibid., 91.
14. See, for example, Robert Nozick, "Socratic Puzzles," *Phronesis* 40, no. 2 (July 1995): 147.
15. Josiah Forshall et al., *The New Testament in English according to the version by John Wycliffe* (Oxford: Clarendon Press, 1879), 445. Accessed December 17, 2015. American Theological

Library Association (ATLA) Historical Monographs Collection: Series 1, EBSCOhost. (Spelling has been modernized by the author.)

16. Scripture taken from *The Message.*

17. Luke Timothy Johnson, *Hebrews: a commentary* (Louisville: Westminster John Knox Press, 2006), 278–279.

Acknowledgements

Throughout my spiritual journey and theological education, I have received encouragement and advice from many wise people. It is not possible to name them all, but I am deeply grateful for each one. Their guidance, kindness and scholarship have made this book possible.

A number of friends have been my companions during the writing of this book. Without their confidence in my purpose and constructive suggestions, my progress from idea to finished manuscript would have been impossible:

Readers for various drafts of the manuscript were Allegra and Jerry Donaldson; Phyllis and Bill Klein; Jan DenBleyker; Susan Anderson; Kathryn O'Connell; Jocelyn Bakkemo; Kathy Kreidler; Kandi Stimson; Regan and Rick Powell; Harvey Powers; and

Margie McCaslin. The encouragement of these friends was essential. Their feedback led to many necessary revisions.

The men's book group from St. Gabriel the Archangel Episcopal Church, Cherry Hills Village, Colorado and the Jasmine Street women's book club took the time to read and discuss the manuscript with me over a period of weeks, and provided the critiques I needed in order to make the final draft a reality.

I particularly appreciate the generous assistance of my friend, Dr. Phyllis Klein. Her creative and editorial gifts greatly enhanced the clarity of the manuscript.

I am deeply grateful to Dr. Larry Ellis, my friend and publisher, whose unflagging enthusiasm and hard work on my behalf enabled this book to see the light of day.

Finally, I owe the congregations and clergy of Ecclesia Church and Resurrection Anglican Fellowship a debt of love. They rejoiced when I rejoiced and wept when I wept. I hold you in my heart.

Barbara Russo
Pentecost, 2016

CPSIA information can be obtained
at www.ICGtesting.com
Printed in the USA
LVOW10s0007040117
519651LV00001B/4/P